NORTH CAROLINA
STATE BOARD OF COMMUNITY COLLEGES
LIBRARIES
FORSYTH TECHNICAL COMMUNITY COLLEGE

SONGS OF A FRIEND

D0840053

Love Lyrics of

Medieval Portugal

Selections from

Cantigas de Amigo

translated by

Barbara Hughes Fowler

THE UNIVERSITY OF

NORTH CAROLINA PRESS

Chapel Hill & London

Songs

OF A FRIEND

DISCARD

LIBRARY
FORSYTH TECHNICAL COMMUNITY COLLEGE
2100 SILAS CREEK PARKWAY
WINSTON-SALEM, NC 27103-5197

© 1996
The University of
North Carolina Press
All rights reserved
Manufactured in the
United States of America

The paper in this book meets
the guidelines for permanence
and durability of the Committee
on Production Guidelines for
Book Longevity of the Council
on Library Resources.

The illustrations appearing in
the text are from Arthur M. Hind,
An Introduction to a History of Woodcut,
2 vols. (London, 1935).

00 99 98 97 96
5 4 3 2 1

Library of Congress
Cataloging-in-Publication Data
Songs of a friend : love lyrics of
medieval Portugal : selections from
Cantigas de amigo / translated by
Barbara Hughes Fowler.
p. cm.
The translations are made from
the edition of J. J. Nunes, Cantigas
d'amigo dos trovadores galego-
portugueses, Coimbra, 1926.
Includes bibliographical references.
ISBN 0-8078-2271-x (cloth : alk.
paper).—ISBN 0-8078-4574-4
(pbk. : alk. paper)
1. Portuguese poetry—To 1500—
Translations into English. 2. Love
poetry, Portuguese—Translations into
English. I. Fowler, Barbara Hughes,
1926– . II. Cantigas d'amigo dos
trovadores galego-portugueses.
English. Selections.
PQ9163.E6S66 1996
869.1'1080354—dc20   95-38532
CIP

69.11
N
96

FOR TERRY

CONTENTS

ACKNOWLEDGMENTS

I wish to thank Mary Lou Daniel, Arnold Rocha, and particularly Joseph Snow for reading my manuscript; they saved me from a number of errors and made other valuable suggestions as well. Since I did not in every instance accept their advice, I must emphasize that I alone am responsible for any errors or infelicities that remain. In addition, I want once more to thank my wonderful editors, Barbara Hanrahan and Ron Maner, at the University of North Carolina Press.

Introduction

Three types of poetry have come down to us from twelfth- and thirteenth-century Portugal. One is the *cantigas de escarnho e de mal dizer* (songs of mockery and slander), verses, often obscene, in which poets hurl invective at a number of phenomena, ranging from military fiascoes and the Crusades to the moral and professional failings of other poets, physical deformities, and the notorious Maria Peres, a promiscuous gambler and camp follower who frequented the court of Alfonso X and was paid for her singing and dancing. This genre derives from the Provençal *sirventês*, or satirical songs. Another is the *cantigas de amor* (songs of love), in which a man sings to a noble and therefore unattainable lady of his highly idealized love for her. This genre owes much to the Provençal troubadour tradition. The third genre—and the focus of this collection—the *cantigas de amigo* (songs of a friend), is more mysterious in origin but seems to stem from a native Galician-Portuguese tradition.[1] In these songs, surprisingly and enchantingly, male poets, assuming a female voice, sing of an ordinary young girl's love for an absent lover or "friend." Often the girl confides in her mother, her sister, or her female friends.

The exact nature of the girl's confidence may vary: in one poem, for example, a young married woman explains to her lover that she cannot meet him because she fears the wrath of her husband, and in another a mother complains to her daughter that she competes with her for a man. Typically, however, in theme the *cantigas de amigo* fall into one of several recognizable categories: *barcarolas*, or sea songs, in which a young girl

---

1. On theories regarding its origin see Frede Jensen, ed. and trans., *Medieval Galician-Portuguese Poetry: An Anthology* (New York, 1992), lxi–lxiii.

misses her lover who has gone to sea; *alvorados*, or dawn songs, in which a girl is reluctant to part with a lover at dawn or, in one instance, goes in the early morning to wash her clothes; *romarias*, or pilgrimage songs, in which a girl goes to a sanctuary to meet a lover; *cantigas de monteiro*, or mountain songs, in which a girl goes to the hills to meet a lover at a fountain where stags (an obvious erotic symbol) come; *bailadas*, or dance songs; or *pastorelas*, or pastoral songs, in which the poet in his own voice quotes the song of a shepherdess. More than five hundred of these songs have come down to us. Since the themes, though worked with infinite variations, are basically quite repetitive, I have selected just under one hundred representative poems to translate.

The poets themselves fall into three groups: the *trovador*, often a nobleman, who composed music and poetry without reward; the *segrel*, often an impoverished knight or squire, who was paid for his work; and the *jogral*, a paid performer of humble birth, who recited either his own or others' poems and played musical instruments as well.

No one is more aware than I that in translating poetry "what is lost is the poetry." In translating from a Romance to a Germanic language the problem is compounded. As a friend has said, "English is so square!" Indeed, I did sometimes feel that I was working with tombstones rather than seashells. There is no way to achieve in English the lilting lyricism of the Portuguese lines, with their fascinating nasals and sibilants that differ so from those of other Romance languages. One can only hope to make an English poem that will give the content if not the lovely sounds of the original. I want simply to give a modern audience some idea of the freshness and charm of these little-known songs, which are in their spontaneous secularism so different from anything else that has come down to us from the Middle Ages.

The Portuguese songs have strict metrical and rhyming patterns.[2] I have made my own formal metrical patterns but have relied upon alliteration and assonance rather than rhyme to make Anglo-Saxon sound patterns. Since my translations are almost line-for-line, they will give the reader an idea of the patterns of the originals, in which one stanza may repeat the previous stanza with the change of only a single word or in which whole lines are repeated in varying patterns to give a fugue-like structure to the entire poem. The refrain, which often undercuts the entire stanza, is an essential component of the *cantigas de amigo*.

I have based my translation on the original text in the edition of J. J. Nunes, *Cantigas d'Amigo dos Trovadores Galego-Portugueses* (Coimbra, 1926). For each poem, I provide identifying numbers from earlier sources: "cv" and "cb" refer to the *Cancioneiro da Vaticana* and the *Cancioneiro da Biblioteca Nacional* respectively, the manuscripts from which Nunes made his edition; "n" refers to Nunes and indicates the number of the poem in his edition.

2. On the versification see Jensen, *Medieval Galician-Portuguese Poetry*, xlviii–lvi.

Afonso Eanes do Coton

CV 411, CB 825, N 232

"Ah, my lover, my light, and my delight,
I see that you are now very sad, and so
I should like to know from you or anyone
what reason there is for you to be so sad."
　　"By God, my lady, I'll tell you one thing:
　　I'm badly off if you don't know the cause."

"You've been very sad for a very long time,
and I know not for what nor even for whom it's so.
Tell me now, and may God grant pardon to you,
what reason there is for you to be so sad."
　　"Oh God, alas, the sorrow of my heart:
　　I'm badly off if you don't know the cause."

"You are sad and I without delight,
because I alone do not know
if it's the grief of love that makes you so
or what reason there is for you to be so sad."
　　"By God, ah, my very pretty lady,
　　I'm badly off if you don't know the cause."

"You are very sad, and I know not
the reason why, but since I see it not,
tell me, and be it not a trouble to you,
what reason there is for you to be so sad."
　　"By God, my lady, O my sorrow and grief,
　　I'm badly off if you don't know the cause."

Afonso Lopes de Baiam

CV 342, CB 740, N 175

They've told me some news of benefit to me,
that my friend has arrived, and if he comes there,
to Holy Mary of Leyras,
I'll go, looking my loveliest, to find if my friend comes there.

They've told me some news that's sweet to me,
that my friend has arrived, and if he goes there,
to Holy Mary of Leyras,
I'll go, looking my loveliest, to find if my friend comes there.

They've told me some news of pleasure to me,
that my friend has arrived, but I, in order to see,
to Holy Mary of Leyras
shall go, looking my loveliest, to find if my friend comes there.

Never with news was a woman so blithe
as I with that, and if he comes there,
to Holy Mary of Leyras,
I'll go, looking my loveliest, to find if my friend comes there.

Afonso Sanches

CV 368, CB 784, N 200

The lovely one would say,
"Ah, God, help me!
How I am wounded by love!
Ah, God, help me!
How I am wounded by love!"

The beautiful one would say,
"Ah, God, help me!
How I am grieved by love!
Ah, God, help me!
How I am wounded by love!

And how I'm wounded by love!
Ah, God, help me!
My beloved does not come!
Ah, God, help me!
How I am wounded by love!

And how I am grieved by love!
Ah, God, help me!
My lover does not come!
Ah, God, help me!
How I am wounded by love!"

Airas Corpancho

CV 265, CB 663, N 117

I thought in my heart I'd make a pilgrimage
to Santiago one day to offer a prayer
and to see my friend there.

If the weather's fine and my mother does not go,
I want to travel, happy, and looking my best,
and to see my friend there.

I'll try very soon to see if I'll be able
to burn my candles with the awful longing I have
and to see my friend there.

Airas Corpancho

CV 259, CB 658, N 92

Lovely mother, I saw my friend
but did not speak with him and so I lost him,
    but now I'm dying of love for him.
    I did not speak because of my disdain;
    I'm dying, mother, for love of him.

If I did him wrong, then I
deserve to suffer because I did not speak with him,
    but now I'm dying of love for him.
    I did not speak because of my disdain;
    I'm dying, mother, for love of him.

Lovely mother, go to beseech him
that he do a good deed and come to see me,
    but now I'm dying of love for him.
    I did not speak because of my disdain;
    I'm dying, mother, for love of him.

Airas Nunes de Santiago

CV 464, CB 881, N 259

"Dance today, my daughter, to please yourself,
before your friend with whom you're so in love."
"I shall dance, mother, since you command me so,
Nevertheless, I notice one thing in you:
that he live but a little pleases you much,
since you ask me to dance before him beautifully."

"I ask you, ah, my daughter, by God, that you dance
before your friend because you're beautiful."
"I shall dance, mother, since you tell me to.
Nevertheless, I notice one thing in you:
that he live but a little gratifies you,
since you ask me to dance before him beautifully."

"By God, my daughter, see to it that you dance
before your friend beneath the pomegranate."
"I shall dance, mother, this particular time.
Nevertheless, I notice one thing in you:
that he live but a little pleases you much,
since you ask me to dance before him beautifully."

"Dance today, my daughter, by Holy Mary,
before your friend who loves you so well."
"I shall dance, mother for you in every way.
Nevertheless, I notice one thing in you:
that he live but a little is what you insist,
since you ask me to dance before him beautifully."

A wedding, from the *Spiegel des menschlichen Lebens*, Augsburg,
ca. 1475–76.

Airas Nunes de Santiago

CV 454, CB 868, 869, 870, N 256

Today I heard a shepherdess sing
as I rode along the river bank,
and the shepherdess was there all alone.
I hid myself that I might hear, and she
very beautifully was singing this song:
    "Under the blossoming green bough
      they toast the wedding of my friend,
      and my eyes weep with love."

And the shepherdess was very pretty,
and she would weep, and she would sing, and I
stole quietly close to approach her
and hear, but I said not a single thing, and she
very beautifully was singing this song:
    "Oh, starling of the filbert tree,
      you sing, but I grieve and die,
      for I suffer from love."

And then I heard the shepherdess sigh,
and she lamented because she was in love,
and she was fashioning a garland of buds;
and then she wept there from deep in her heart,
and she very beautifully sang this song:
    "How greatly I grieve to love my friend
      and dare not see him, but I
      shall sit beneath the filbert tree."

After the shepherdess had made her wreath,
she went, singing, slowly on her way,
and I turned at once upon my road,
since I had no desire to displease her,
and the shepherdess sang this song beautifully:

———

"Beside the river went the girl,
singing of love. 'How will she sleep,
the one in love, O pretty bud?'"

Bernal de Bonaval

CV 731, CB 1140, N 361

The pretty one in Bonaval spoke thus:
"God, where has he gone from here, my friend
    of Bonaval?

I believe that he is pained of heart, for he
was not with me at the dedication
    of Bonaval.

Since I have not his message with me, I shall
not be able to part happily yet
    from Bonaval.

Since his message has not come to me here,
I came much more happily than I go
    from Bonaval."

Bernal de Bonaval

CV 729, CB 1138, N 359

Since you tell me, friend,
that you love me more
than all the women in the world,
say, by our Lord,
    if you love me so much,
    how can you go from here?

And since you say that you
can't love another so much,
tell me, ah my friend,
if God protects you,
    if you love me so much,
    how can you go from here?

And since I hear you say
that you don't love another
so much, tell me now, if God
takes you from Bonaval,
    if you love me so much,
    how can you go from here?

Since I have always heard
that when a man adores
a woman, he can't depart from her,
it will grieve me not to know
    if you love me so much,
    how can you go from here?

Bernal de Bonaval

cv 728, cb 1137, n 358

"Ah, my lovely one, if you please,
whom do you await far from the town?"
"I've come to await my friend."

"Ah, my lovely one, if you will,
whom do you expect far from the town?"
"I've come to await my friend."

"Whom do you await far from the town?"
"I will tell you that since you ask it of me.
I've come to await my friend."

"Whom do you expect far from the town?"
"I will tell you that since you do not know.
I've come to await my friend."

Dom Dinis

CV 172, CB 569, N 20

The lovely girl
arose at earliest dawn,
and goes to wash her camisoles
    at the river swirl.
She goes to wash them at earliest dawn.

The elegant girl
arose at earliest dawn,
and goes to wash her petticoats
    at the river swirl.
She goes to wash them at earliest dawn.

She goes to wash her camisoles.
She rose at earliest dawn.
The wind is scattering them
    at the river swirl.
She goes to wash them at earliest dawn.

She goes to wash her petticoats.
She rose at earliest dawn.
The wind has born them off
    at the river swirl.
She goes to wash them at earliest dawn.

The wind is scattering them.
She rose at earliest dawn.
At dawn she was enraged
    at the river swirl.
She goes to wash them at earliest dawn.

The wind has born them off.
She rose at earliest dawn.
At dawn she was furious
        at the river swirl.
She goes to wash them at earliest dawn.

Dom Dinis

CV 171, CB 568, N 19

O blossoms of the verdant pine,
if you have news of my friend?
    O God, where is he?

O blossoms of the verdant bough,
if you have news of my beloved?
    O God, where is he?

If you have news of my friend,
who lied about what he promised to me?
    O God, where is he?

If you have news of my beloved,
who lied about what he swore to me?
    O God, where is he?

You ask me about that friend of yours,
and I tell you that he is well and alive.
    O God, where is he?

You ask me about that friend of yours,
and I tell you that he is alive and well.
    O God, where is he?

And I tell you that he is well and alive,
and will be with you before very long.
    O God, where is he?

And I tell you that he is alive and well
and will be with you now very soon.
    O God, where is he?

Dom Dinis

CV 195, CB 592, N 43

My lovely mother,
I'm going to the dance
of love.

My laudable mother,
I'm going to the ball
of love.

I'm going to the dance
that's happening in the town
of love.

I'm going to the ball
that's happening in the house
of love.

That's happening in the town—
his whom I've much desired—
of love.

That's happening in the house—
his whom I've dearly loved—
of love.

His whom I've much desired.
They'll summon me, bedecked,
to love.

His for whom I've dearly longed.
They'll summon me to the oath
of love.

———

Dom Dinis

CV 168, CB 565, N 16

I've had a fine day, my friend,
since I have your message with me,
lovely me!

I've seen a fine day, my love,
since I have your message with me,
lovely me!

Since I have your message with me,
I pray to God and I say,
lovely me!

Since I have your message with me
I willingly pray to God,
lovely me!

I pray to God and I speak
for that friend of mine,
lovely me!

I willingly pray to God
for that love of mine,
lovely me!

For that friend of mine,
whom I'd see with me,
lovely me!

For that beloved of mine
whom I'd have here now,
lovely me!

Dom Dinis

CV 173, CB 570, N 21

My beloved and my friend,
 may God protect you!
See the blossoming pine.
 Prepare to go.

My friend and my beloved,
 may God protect you!
See the blossoming branch.
 Prepare to go.

See the blossoming pine,
 may God protect you!
Saddle the little bay.
 Prepare to go.

See the blossoming branch,
 may God protect you!
Saddle the beautiful horse.
 Prepare to go.

Saddle the little bay,
 may God protect you!
Hasten now, my friend.
 Prepare to go.

Saddle the beautiful horse,
 may God protect you!
Hasten now, my beloved.
 Prepare to go.

Dom Dinis

CV 170, CB 567, N 18

Of what are you dying, daughter, of body so fair?
Mother, I'm dying for the love my friend bestowed.
It's dawn, and quickly he goes.

Of what are you dying, daughter, of body so lithe?
Mother, I'm dying for the love my lover bestowed.
It's dawn, and quickly he goes.

Mother, I'm dying for the love my friend bestowed
whenever I look at this sash I tie for his love.
It's dawn, and quickly he goes.

Mother, I'm dying for the love my lover bestowed
whenever I look at this sash that I wear for his love.
It's dawn, and quickly he goes.

Whenever I look at this sash that I tie for his love
and remember, pretty me, how he spoke with me.
It's dawn, and quickly he goes.

Whenever I look at this sash that I wear for his love
and remember, pretty me, how both of us spoke.
It's dawn, and quickly he goes.

Dom Dinis

CV 169, CB 566, N 17

Mother, my friend hasn't come,
and today is the time fulfilled.
O mother, I'm dying of love!

Mother, my love hasn't come,
and today is the time gone by.
O mother, I'm dying of love!

And today is the time fulfilled.
Why did the traitor lie?
O mother, I'm dying of love!

And today is the time gone by.
Why did the perjurer lie?
O mother, I'm dying of love!

That the traitor lied
deliberately grieves me.
O mother, I'm dying of love!

That the perjurer lied
purposely grieves me.
Oh, mother, I'm dying of love!

Dom Dinis

CV 189, CB 586, N 37

I saw you, mother, speaking with my friend
today, and I listened very pleasurably,
for I saw him happily rise from beside you
and believe that God does benefit to me;
    since he departed happily from there,
    it cannot be that it's not good for me.

Happily he rose and laughing went,
a thing that he'd not done for a long time,
but since this happened just now, may I, happy,
await to see if God favors me;
    since he departed happily from there,
    it cannot be that it's not good for me.

His eyes have encountered mine since that time
that you saw him take his departure from you
and turn happily and laughing away,
and I have therefore pleasure in my heart;
    since he departed happily from there,
    it cannot be that it's not good for me.

Although I know nothing of your talk,
I've great pleasure, mother, from what I saw.

Dom Dinis

CV 188, CB 585, N 36

I should like to speak with pleasure to you,
O my friend and my beloved,
but I dare not today to speak with you,
for I greatly fear the angry one.
Angry be God with him who gave me to him!

I struggle in thoughts for a thousand ways
to tell to you what troubles me,
but I dare not today to speak with you,
for I greatly fear the cruel one.
Cruel be God to him who gave me to him!

I have suffered much, my friend,
to tell you of my secret grief,
but I dare not today to speak with you,
for I greatly fear the wrathful one.
Wrathful be God with him who gave me to him!

Lord of my heart, unhappy you are
because I must live with whom I live,
but I dare not today to speak with you,
for I greatly fear the scornful one.
Scornful be God with him who gave me to him!

Dom Dinis

CV 150, CB 547, N 3

I saw singing today
of love in a beautiful meadow
a beautiful shepherdess
whose appearance surpassed
any I'd seen, and so
I spoke to her thus:
"Lady, I'm yours to command."

She turned angrily then
when she heard me speak and said,
"Go away, good sir.
Who was it who brought you here
to come and hinder me
from singing that song composed
by him with whom I'm in love?"

"Since you command me to go,"
I said to her, "I must,
but I shall serve you always,
my lady, because my love
for you forces me to,
so I'm at your command
and yours will eternally be."

Then she said, "There's no
profit for you in what
you say, nor pleasure for me
to hear, but rather disgust
and pain. My heart's not,
nor will it be, in faith,
anyone's but whom I love."

"Nor will mine," said I,
   to her "part from you
   to whom it believes it belongs."
"Mine," said she, "will be
   where it always was and is,
   and I don't care one whit for you."

Dom Dinis

CV 102, CB 519, N 1

A shepherdess was lamenting
much, the other day
and talking with herself,
and she would weep and say
with the love overwhelming her,
"By God, it was a sorry day
    I saw you, ah, my love!"

And that one was lamenting like
a woman who'd grieved and sorrowed
from the day that she was born
although she'd suffered nothing at all,
and so she would constantly say as she wept,
"You're nothing at all if not the cause
    of my grief, ah, my love!"

Love gave sorrows to her
that were nothing to her if not death,
and she lay among some blossoms,
and she said with enormous grief,
"May evil come to you wherever
you go, for you're nothing at all if not
    my death, ah, my love!"

Estevam Coelho

CV 321, CB 720, N 155

The lovely girl sat twisting her silk,
her soft voice beautifully chanting
songs of a friend.

The lovely girl was weaving her silk,
her soft voice beautifully singing
songs of a friend.

"By God of the Cross, lady, I know
you grieve for love, you chant so well
songs of a friend.

By God of the Cross, lady, I know
you grieve for love, you sing so well
songs of a friend."

"You've eaten a vulture that you guess."[1]

1. It was supposed that by eating the flesh of a vulture one could guess a
person's thoughts or foretell the future.

Fernan Frojaz

CV 390, CB 806, N 218

"My friend, I must ask
since you weep,
why do you grieve?"
    "My lady, you I will tell:
    I am in love, and a man in love,
    painful though it be, must grieve."

Fernan Gonçalvez de Seabra

CV 338, CB 737, N 171

Although I asked of my friend
that he not go, not even for me did he fail
to abandon me, and when he returned here
and saw how very angry I was with him,
  he wept so much and with such heart
  that I wept then for the pain on his part.

I asked him that he weep
no more, for I pardoned him, and I promised that
for his abandonment of me I'd seek
not a single thing, but before I could ask him that
  he wept so much and with such heart
  that I wept then for the pain on his part.

He swore to me that he
did not suppose that I'd suffer so much from that;
otherwise, better for him to kill
himself. When he saw my anger with him,
  he wept so much and with such heart
  that I wept then for the pain on his part.

From Jean d'Arras, *Melusina*, Strassburg, ca. 1478.

Fernan Rodriguez de Calheiros

CV 233, CB 632, N 66

Mother, there passed through here a cavalier.
He left me in love to suffering.
 Ah, mother, I have his love,
  and if I do,
  I sought the pangs
  but gave him mine.
 Ah, mother, I pine for his love.

Mother, there passed through here a nobleman.
He left me to grieving, as I do.
 Ah, mother, I have his love,
  and if I do,
  I sought the pangs
  but gave him mine.
 Ah, mother, I pine for his love.

Mother, there passed through here who shouldn't have.
He left me to grieving, but let it go!
 Ah, mother, I have his love.
  and if I do,
  I sought the pangs
  but gave him mine.
 Ah, mother, I pine for his love.

Fernan Rodriguez de Calheiros

CV 227, CB 626, N 60

I have lost, I think, my mother, my friend. Although
he saw me, he didn't seek to speak with me,
    and my pride has driven him away from me
    who did that that he had forbidden me.

Although he saw me, he didn't seek to speak,
and I feigned to take no notice of his reproach,
    and my pride has driven him away from me
    who did that that he had forbidden me.

And I feigned to take no notice of his reproach.
What good does it do me now to speak of it?
    And my pride has driven him away from me
    who did that that he had forbidden me.

I trusted so in the depth of his love for me
that I wasn't circumspect in what I did,
    and my pride has driven him away from me
    who did that that he had forbidden me.

I wasn't circumspect in what I did
and caused sorrow to him who caused me none,
    and my pride has driven him away from me
    who did that that he had forbidden me.

I caused sorrow to him who did me none,
and now my folly has redounded on me,
    and my pride has driven him away from me
    who did that that he had forbidden me.

Fernan Rodriguez de Calheiros

CV 234, CB 632, N 67

My friend said to me
when he went on his way
that I should not be sad for him,
that he would soon return,
    and I wonder only
    why this delay.

My friend said to me
when he went away from here
that I should not be sad for him,
but he is late and does not come to me,
    and I wonder only
    why this delay.

That I should not be sad for him,
that he would soon return,
but I grieve that he is late,
as Holy Mary knows, Mother of God,[2]
    and I wonder only
    why this delay.

That I should not be sad for him,
but he is late and does not come to me,
but that is not because
he does not love me very much,
    and I wonder only
    why this delay.

2. "Mother of God" is not in the original text. I added it for the sake of the meter.

———

The fowler, from *Dyalogus Creaturarum*, Gouda, 1480.

Fernando Esquio

CV 902, CB 1298, N 506

Let us go, my sister, let us go to sleep
on the banks of the lake, where I have seen
my friend go to hunt birds.

Let us go, my sister, let us go to play
on the banks of the lake, where I have seen
my friend go to hunt birds.

On the banks of the lake where I have seen,
wounding the birds with the bow in his hands,
my friend who goes to hunt birds.

Since I have seen on the banks of the lake,
drawing the bow in his hand at the birds,
my friend who goes to hunt birds.

Wounding the birds with the bow in his hand;
he allows the carolers to live,
my friend who goes to hunt birds.

Drawing his bow in his hand at the birds;
he seeks not to kill the carolers,
my friend who goes to hunt birds.

Joam Airas de Santiago

CV 614, CB 1024, N 300

My friend speaks as well as he can
about me and my appearance,
and those who know that he speaks thus
believe that I should thank him for that,
>but I don't thank him for a thing that he says,
>because I know very well how pretty I am.

He calls me lovely, he calls me Lady,
and says who sees me will call me lovely
and believes that thus he proves his passion
and that I should be grateful to him for that,
>but I don't thank him for a thing that he says,
>because I know very well how pretty I am.

He speaks well of me in his songs,
and rightly. I'll tell you another thing.
Those who hear him praising me
believe that I should thank him for that,
>but I don't thank him for a thing that he says,
>because I know very well how pretty I am.

Because were I not very pretty, he'd not say
even a single one of those things that he says.

The birds, from Bartholomaeus Anglicus, *Propriétaire des Choses*, Lyon, ca. 1485–86.

Joam Airas de Santiago

CV 554, CB 967, N 280

Through the grove of Crexente
I saw a shepherdess go
far from the populace,
raising her voice to sing
and covering herself with her cloak
when the rays of the sun appeared
along the banks of the Sar.

And the birds that flew when dawn
appeared were singing, all
of them, of love throughout
the branches round about,
but I know not who was there
who could think other
than entirely of love.

There I quietly stood,
longing to speak but daring
not. With fear I said,
"My lady, I shall speak
a little with you; if
you'll listen, I'll go when you
command and not remain."

"Sir, by Holy Mary,
be no longer here,
but go on your way,
and behave prudently too,
since those who arrive here
and learn that you were about
will say that more went on."

Joam d'Avoin

CV 269, CB 666, N 101

Did you see, mother, when my friend
promised that he would come to speak with me?
    Do you suppose that he will come today?

Did you see how he promised he'd never receive,
if he did not come, any benefit from me?
    Do you suppose that he will come today?

Did you see the oaths that he swore to me
that he'd come unless a prisoner or dead?
    Do you suppose that he will come today?

Did you see the oaths that he swore just there
that he would come and that he swore by me?
    Do you suppose that he will come today?

Joam d'Avoin

CV 278, CB 676, N 110

I rode the other day
along the road from France,
and a shepherdess sang
with another three, and not
to keep you in suspense,
I'll tell you everything
that shepherdess said
to the others as advice:
> "Never should a woman have faith in her friend,
> since mine left and did not speak with me."

"Shepherdess, you say
nothing of worth," another
said. "If he left this time,
he'll come again and tell
you why he did not speak
with you, my elegant one;
more sensible for you
to sing, as I do:
> 'God, if my friend came now
> he would take great pleasure with me.'"

Joam Baveca

CV 832, CB 1227, N 440

"Daughter, I'd like, if you please, to know
about you and your friend one thing:
how is it with you and how does it go?"
"Mother, I'm willing to tell you that
    I love him well as he does me,
      and I tell you truly, there's nothing more."

"Daughter, I know not whether there's more,
but I see you talking always with him,
and I see you weep, and he weeps too."
"Mother, I'll give you no other reply:
    I love him well as he does me,
      and I tell you truly, there's nothing more."

"Daughter, if you refuse me, I'll be
aggrieved, for if anything more's been done,
we'll be in need of further advice."
"Mother, I've told you all that there is:
    I love him well as he does me,
      and I tell you truly, there's nothing more."

Joam Baveca

CV 830, CB 1225, N 438

My friend, I know you've reason to compose
verses of love for me, and now
I see that they reprove you for that,
but never may God give help to me
if I don't henceforth give reason to you
  to compose songs of a friend.

And since they see fit to pretend that you
compose for one who never since
her birth did you a kindly thing,
I tell you that from here forth
I wish to give you reason of love
  to compose songs of a friend.

And God knows, I did not intend
to do a thing like this for you,
but since they keep you from composing,
you see the power they have, for I
shall find a way to allow you
  to compose songs of a friend.

Joam de Cangas

CV 875, CB 1269, N 482

My friend, if you love me very much, go
to San Mamed' and you will see me there;
   don't deceive me today, my friend.

Since you're not able to say a thing to me here,
go where you will be at leisure with me;
   don't deceive me today, my friend.

I shall be with you at San Mamed' by the Sea
in the chapel there, if God permits me;
   don't deceive me today, my friend.

Joam Garcia Guilhade

CV 357, CB 754, N 189

Every single time that my friend comes here
he says to me, my dears, that he's losing his mind
over me and that he's dying because of me,
but I know very well that this is not so,
    because I've never seen him eager to die,
    nor do I ever observe that he's insane.

He weeps much and undertakes to swear
that he is mad and seeks to make me know
that he is dying for me, but since he hasn't,
I know very well that he's malingering,
    because I've never seen him eager to die,
    nor do I ever observe that he's insane.

Now let us see what he will say to us,
since he arrives alive and is not mad.
I'll say to him, "Haven't you died of love?"
May he acquit himself of his vow to me,
    because I've never seen him eager to die,
    nor do I ever observe that he's insane.

    He'll never again make me believe
    that he dies for me, unless he does!

Joam Garcia Guilhade

CV 431, CB 845, N 245

My ladies, they caused my friend
to go from here to my grief,
and he who planned this grief for me,
may God reward him thus for that:
    that there come to him as there came to me
    sorrow whence he may long for joy.

And may he see himself in love's irresistible hold,
and there be no help for him,
and for that one who caused my grief,
may our Lord reward him thus:
    that there come to him as there came to me
    sorrow whence he may long for joy.

Because they made him go
to wrong me and my eyes,
for him who caused my grief, may God
show to him soon equal grief:
    that there come to him as there came to me
    sorrow whence he may long for joy.

May there come to him sorrow for that
from God, from me, from anyone.

Joam Garcia Guilhade

CV 344, CB 742, N 177

By God, my friends, what is to be
since that world is worth not a thing
if a friend cares not for his love?
And that world, what is it now,
since love has no power there.
What is a fine appearance worth
or a lovely figure to anyone?

You see why I speak this way:
because there's not a king in the world
who'd see the figure that I have
and who'd not die therefore for me.
Furthermore, my eyes are green! But
my friend didn't see me just now
and passed by here without a glance.

But the lady who happens to have a friend,
from today on (may she believe it,
by God) let her eyes not strain themselves,
for they have no necessity from today,
for someone else has seen my eyes
just now and my fine figure. He comes
and goes just as it pleases him.

But since a good figure is worthless
and a fine appearance too,
let us appear just as we please!

Joam Lopez d'Ulhoa

CV 301, CB 700, N 132

I never sleep at all,
but wonder about my friend.
Because he tarries so,
has he another love?
    If he's not mine, I'd seek
    today to die.

I have that always in mind.
I know not if he's mine.
Because he tarries so,
does he desire another?
    If he's not mine, I'd seek
    today to die.

If so, he does me wrong.
By God, he murders me.
Because he tarries so,
does he gaze at another's face?
    If he's not mine, I'd seek
    today to die.

For it would cost me dear
to live another day.

Joam Lopez d'Ulhoa

CV 297, CB 696, N 128

Ah, God, where is my friend
who's sent no message to me,
although he promised me
that unless he were afflicted
        by death, he'd come
        as soon as he could?

When he parted from me,
he wept and made me a vow
and told me the very day
that unless he were tormented
        to death, he'd come
        as soon as he could.

But now the time is past
when he said that he would come
and when he'd sworn to me
that unless he suffered even
        from death, he'd come
        as soon as he could.

And if I'd known other than that,
I'd never have loved him so well!

Joam Nunes Camanez

CV 255, CB 654, N 88

Go, ah, my mother, to see my beloved who
is suffering because he does not speak with me,
    and I will go with you, if you wish.

He suffers so that he will die not seeing me.
Go, my mother, to see him to save him from that,
    and I will go with you, if you wish.

Because he loves me in his heart to the brink of death,
go see him, my mother, and then at least he will live,
    and I will go with you, if you wish.

Joam Nunes Camanez

CV 252, CB 651, N 85

"If I, my daughter, go
to see your friend, because
he's dying of love for you
and can no longer live,
    will you go together with me?"
    "By God, my mother, I will."

"Since he desires you
so much that he can't be cured,
tell me one thing, for
I wish to go to him there:
    will you go together with me?"
    "By God, my mother, I will."

"Since I've seen him grieve
and die for you there,
my daughter, and since I go
and no one else with me,
    will you go together with me?"
    "By God, my mother, I will."

DISCARD

LIBRARY
FORSYTH TECHNICAL COMMUNITY COLLEGE
2100 SILAS CREEK PARKWAY
WINSTON-SALEM, NC 27103-5197

Joam Servando

CV 742, CB 1149, N 372

I, for all my grace, am sad, I tell
you truly so, because they don't allow me to see my friend;
   they can guard me now,
but they'll not keep me from loving him.

Although they beat me the other day for him,
I went to San Servando to see if I could see him;
   they can guard me now,
but they'll not keep me from loving him.

Although they hope to keep me from seeing him,
it's impossible that this thing they do come to be;
   they can guard me now,
but they'll not keep me from loving him.

And they can guard me well,
but they'll not keep me from loving him.

Joam Servando

CV 738, 749, CB 1146 bis, N 368

Now there go to San Servando
damsels to make a pilgrimage,
but they don't allow me to go
with them, for I would straightway go,
  because my friend is going there.

If I were in such a company
of damsels, I'd be chaperoned,
but my mother didn't want me today
to make that pilgrimage with them,
  because my friend is going there,

Such a pilgrimage of damsels
goes there as has no equal, and I
would be going with them now,
but they don't wish to permit me,
  because my friend is going there.

May my mother never see me
if I am not avenged because
I cannot go to San Servando
today and she keeps me chaperoned,
  because my friend is going there.

Joam Soarez Coelho

CV 291, CB 689, N 122

I went, my mother, to wash my hair
at the fountain, and I was pleased with it,
and with myself, lovely me!

I went, my mother, to wash my locks
at the fountain, and I was pleased with them,
and with myself, lovely me!

At the fountain I was pleased with them,
and there I found my lord of them
and of me, lovely me!

Before I went away from there
I was pleased with what he said to me,
and about me, lovely me!

Joam Soarez Coelho

CV 290, CB 688, N 121

Ah, my friend, if you understand
the pleasure of all you love in the world,
    take me away with you, my friend.

That you don't abandon your pretty one
to live as I live, troubled, today,
    take me away with you, my friend.

By God, accept compassion from me;
you'd live better with me than alone;
    take me away with you, my friend.

Joam Soarez Coelho

CV 288, CB 686, N 119

Do you see, friends, that my suitor comes
and has sent to speak with me and asks
that I permit him to talk to me,
but of such a promise I know not a thing.
    It grieves me that he sent to speak to me,
    and do for him what I know not how to do.

Because, although I'd be pleased,
and am greatly concerned in my heart about
permitting him, if God forgives,
I'll not permit, since I wouldn't know how.
    It grieves me that he sent to speak to me,
    and do for him what I know not how to do.

Since I've never spoken with any man—
may our Lord not help me if I lie—
since I was born, nor am I skilled
in talk like that that I've never done or know.
    It grieves me that he sent to speak to me,
    and do for him what I know not how to do.

Joam Soarez Coelho

CV 282, CB 680, N 113

Friend, you complain of me
that I don't speak with you,
but, as much as I know
of you, you know no part
    of what I'd suffer, my friend,
    if you should speak with me.

Nor of how threatened I was
and wounded one day by being
parted from you, nor do
you know a single thing
    of what I'd suffer, my friend,
    if you should speak with me.

As soon as you know about
the evil, much and excessive,
they contrive for me, if I
see you, you'll thank me for
    what I'd suffer, my friend,
    if you should speak with me.

But still if you wish that I
see and speak with you,
you simply don't understand
if you don't know in advance
    what I'd suffer my friend,
    if you should speak with me.

Studies of trees, from Konrad von Megenburg, *Buch der Natur*, Augsburg, 1475.

Joam Zorro

CV 761, CB 1158, N 390

Let us dance now, by God, O lovely ones,
beneath those flowering filbert trees,
and whoever is lovely as we are lovely,
if she is in love with a friend,
beneath those flowering filbert trees
will come to dance.

Let us dance now, by God, O laudable ones,
beneath those flowering filbert trees,
and whoever is lauded as we are lauded,
if she is in love with a friend,
beneath those spreading filbert trees
will come to dance.

Joam Zorro

CV 755, CB 1153, N 384

The king of Portugal
ordered boats to be made,
and there will go in the boats
with me, my daughter, our friend.

The king of Portugal
ordered boats to be built,
and there will go in the boats
with me, my daughter, our friend.

He ordered boats to be made
and placed them in the sea,
and there will go in the boats
with me, my daughter, our friend.

He ordered boats to be built
and put them in the sea,
and there will go in the boats
with me, my daughter, our friend.

Joam Zorro

CV 753, CB 1150, N 382

Along the river bank
I saw the boat being rowed,
and I rejoice in the river bank!

Along the river bank
I saw the barque being rowed,
and I rejoice in the river bank!

I saw the boat being rowed
and there my friend goes,
and I rejoice in the river bank!

I saw the barque being rowed
and there my lover goes,
and I rejoice in the river bank!

Where my friend goes
he wants me also to go,
and I rejoice in the river bank!

Where my lover goes
he wants me much to go,
and I rejoice in the river bank!

From Thomas Lirer, *Chronica von allen Königen und Kaisern*, Ulm, ca. 1486.

Joam Zorro

CV 759, CB 1157, N 388

Down to the river and sea
I, your beloved, shall go,
where the king rigs his ship,
my love, I'll go with you.

Down to the river and sea
I, your beloved, shall go,
where the kings rigs his barque,
my love, I'll go with you.

Where the king rigs his ship
I, your beloved, shall go,
to escort the virgin girl,
my love, I'll go with you.

Where the king rigs his barque
I, your beloved, shall go,
to escort the noble girl,
my love, I'll go with you.

Joam Zorro

CV 758, CB 1156, N 387

The king launches his boats in the rapid stream.
If she has a friend, may God reveal him to her.
He goes there, O mother, where
I long for him.

The king launches his boats in the Estremadura.
If she has a friend, may God return him to her.
He goes there, O mother, where
I long for him.

Joam Zorro

CV 754, CB 1151, 1152, N 383

In Lisbon upon the sea
I ordered new barques to be made.
Ah, my lovely lady!

In Lisbon upon the beach
I ordered new barques to be built.
Ah, my lovely lady!

I ordered new barques to be made
and ordered them put in the sea.
Ah, my lovely lady!

I ordered new barques to be built
and ordered them placed in the sea.
Ah, my lovely lady!

Joam Zorro

CV 757, CB 1155, N 386

Along the bank of the stream
went the young girl,
singing of love:
"Let them come in the ships
down the stream,
under full sail!"

Along the bank of the deep
went the noble girl,
singing of love:
"Let them come in the ships
down the stream,
under full sail!"

Joam Zorro

CV 751, CB 1148, N 380

If you could see the lovely one walk,
as I have seen her, afflicted by love,
and so in love,
that weeping thus she spoke:
"O love, allow me today
to rest beneath the bough,
then afterward come with me
to find my friend."

If you could see the lovely one walk,
as I have seen her, weeping for love
and speaking, beseeching,
complaining of love:
"O love, allow me today
to rest beneath the bough,
then afterward come with me
to find my friend."

If you could see her walking and making
lament for the love of her friend,
weeping always
with love and speaking thus:
"O love, allow me today
to rest beneath the bough,
then afterward come with me
to find my friend."

Julião Bolseiro

CV 777, CB 1171, N 400

You treat me badly, ah, my daughter,
because I wish to have a friend,
and since I am in fear of you,
and I have none, no one for me,
    may you have no favor from me,
    and may God give you, my daughter,
    a daughter who uses you thus,
    a daughter who uses you thus.

Surely you know that without a friend
no woman was ever exuberant,
and since you do not allow me
to have a friend, my pretty daughter,
    may you have no favor from me,
    and may God give you, my daughter,
    a daughter who uses you thus,
    a daughter who uses you thus.

Because I do not have my friend,
I don't have a thing that I desire;
since it happened to me through you,
my daughter, that him I do not see,
    may you have no favor from me,
    and may God give you, my daughter,
    a daughter who uses you thus,
    a daughter who uses you thus.

Through you, my daughter, I lost my friend.
For that I endure great suffering,
and since you took him away from me,
and since I'm prettier than you,

may you have no favor from me,
and may God give you, my daughter,
a daughter who uses you thus,
a daughter who uses you thus.

Julião Bolseiro

CV 782, CB 1176, N 405

Those nights that God made so long
on a day somber for me so that
I could not sleep through them—why,
oh why, didn't he make them such
    in the time that my friend
    was wont to speak with me?

Since God made them so very long
and I cannot sleep, I'm suffering.
And since they are excessive, I'd
have asked another occasion for them
    in the time that my friend
    was wont to speak with me.

Why did God make them so long,
immeasurable and so immense,
that I am unable to sleep through them?
Why did he not make them such
    in the time that my friend
    was wont to speak with me?

Juliâo Bolseiro

CV 771, CB 1165, N 394

Without my lover I'm here alone.
My eyes scarcely close in sleep.
I pray to God with all my heart for the light,
but he absolutely refuses to send it to me.
    But if I could be with my beloved,
    the light would now be mine.

When I slept with my lover, the night seemed not
even a moment long, but now
the night arrives and lasts forevermore,
and the light never comes, nor does the day appear.
    But if I could be with my beloved,
    the light would now be mine.

But now it seems that as long as my lord
and my light remain with me, the day
immediately breaks but gives me no delight,
and now the night arrives and waxes long.
    But if I could be with my beloved,
    the light would now be mine.

"Our Father," I pray hundreds of times,
that He who died on the true cross,
show to me very soon the light. Instead,
he shows me nights as long as Advent's span.
    But if I could be with my beloved,
    the light would now be mine.

Julião Bolseiro

CV 772, CB 1166, N 395

From yesterday's night they could have made
three long nights, as my thought goes,
but in today's I had much joy,
    because my lover came,
and before I could send to say a thing to him,
the light broke and was immediately mine.

Yesterday, because I went
to bed alone, the night was long,
but today's little resembled it,
    because my lover came,
and as soon as he began to speak with me,
the light broke and was immediately mine.

I began yesterday to have
concern as the night began to grow,
but today's was not at all like that,
    because my lover came,
and I, speaking with him, took great delight:
the light broke and was immediately mine.

Juliâo Bolseiro

CV 774, CB 1168, N 397

In new boats my friend has gone from here,
and I see the boats come, and I believe that there comes here,
   my mother, my friend.

Let us wait, ah, mother, I'll love you always,
since I see the boats come, and I believe that there comes here,
   my mother, my friend.

I'm not mistaken, my mother, in my opinion,
since there couldn't live elsewhere long without me,
   my mother, my friend.

Julião Bolseiro

CV 773, CB 1167, N 396

I saw today, my mother, my friend, who sent
to me urgently to ask for that,
and so I know that he loves me very much,
but, you know, my mother, since he has seen me with him,
     he's been so joyous that since I was born,
     I've never seen in a man with a woman such joy.

When I arrived, he was weeping continuously,
nor did he allow his heart any rest at all,
worrying whether I'd come or not come,
but when he saw me there, he kindled his hope:
     he's been so joyous that since I was born,
     I've never seen in a man with a woman such joy.

And since it was God's will that I be where
he'd see me and said, my mother, what I'd tell you,
"Here, I see, comes all the joy in the world
that I have," and you know, mother, since he said that,
     he's been so joyous that since I was born,
     I've never seen in a man with a woman such joy.

Lopo

CV 858, CB 1259, N 465

By God, I ask you, mother, to tell me
what I've deserved of you that you keep me so
    from going to San Leuter to speak with my friend.

Do me now as much ill as you can
because you'll not keep me, although you try,
    from going to San Leuter to speak with my friend.

I've never done a thing that I shouldn't have
to you, but I'm powerless, you keep me so
    from going to San Leuter to speak with my friend.

Lopo

CV 857, CB 1252, N 464

"Daughter, if you please, tell
what troubles you."
    "My love does not allow me leisure."

"Daughter, if you see fit,
tell me, don't lie."
    "My love does not allow me leisure."

"Tell me, since I command you,
why do you weep?"
    "My love does not allow me leisure."

"By Saint Leuter, I tell you,
I grieve for my friend.
    My love does not allow me leisure."

Lourenço

CV 869, CB 1264, N 476

My confidante, since I have seen my friend,
he is dying for me, and I am
    his inamorata.

Since I have seen and spoken first with him,
he is dying for me, and I have remained
    his inamorata.

Since we've seen one another, it's thus with us:
he is dying for me, and I am therefore
    his inamorata.

Since we've seen one another, look what befalls:
he is dying for me, and I am quite
    his inamorata.

Martin Codax

CV 890, CB 1284, N 497

O waves that I've come to see,
if you know, tell to me
    why my love lingers
    without me.

O waves that I've come to view,
if you know, reveal to me
    why my love lingers
    without me.

Martin Codax

CV 888, CB 1282, N 495

All you who know how to love a friend,
hurry with me to the sea of Vigo,
    and we shall bathe in the waves.

All you who know how to love a lover,
hurry with me to the turbulent sea,
    and we shall bathe in the waves.

Hurry with me to the sea of Vigo,
and we shall see my friend there,
    and we shall bathe in the waves.

Hurry with me to the turbulent sea,
and we shall see my lover there,
    and we shall bathe in the waves.

Martin Codax

CV 886, CB 1280, N 493

My beautiful sister, come hurry with me
to the church of Vigo beside the turbulent sea,
    and we shall marvel at the waves.

My beautiful sister, come hurry, please,
to the church of Vigo beside the tumultuous sea,
    and we shall marvel at the waves.

To the church of Vigo beside the turbulent sea,
and there will come here, mother, my friend,
    and we shall marvel at the waves.

To the church of Vigo beside the tumultuous sea,
and there will come here, my mother, my love,
    and we shall marvel at the waves.

Martin Codax

cv 884, cb 1278, n 491

Waves of the sea of Vigo,
if you have seen my friend!
    Oh, God, may he come soon!

Waves of the rising sea,
if you have seen my friend!
    Oh, God, may he come soon!

If you have seen my friend,
him for whom I sigh!
    Oh, God, may he come soon!

If you have seen my love,
him for whom I pine,
    Oh, God, may he come soon!

Martin Codax

CV 889, CB 1283, N 496

Inside the sanctuary of Vigo
the lovely girl was dancing:
   I am in love!

Inside the sanctuary of Vigo
the elegant girl was dancing:
   I am in love!

Where the lovely girl was dancing,
she who never had a friend:
   I am in love!

The elegant girl was dancing,
she who never had a lover:
   I am in love!

She who never had a friend
except in the sanctuary of Vigo:
   I am in love!

She who never had a lover
except in the sanctuary of Vigo:
   I am in love!

Martin de Ginzo

CV 876, CB 1270, N 483

How troubled I am,
mother, on behalf of my friend,
since he's sent me a message
that he's going on campaign!
In anguish I live.

How troubled I am,
mother, on behalf of my love,
since he's sent me a message
that he's going into combat!
In anguish I live.

Since he's sent me a message
that he's going on campaign,
to Saint Cecilia I speak
from the very depth of my heart:
In anguish I live.

Since he's sent me a message
that he's going into combat,
to Saint Cecilia I say
from the very depth of my heart:
In anguish I live.

Martin de Ginzo

CV 883, CB 1277, N 490

She of the charming appearance
bade him strike the tambourine.
   Lovely, I'm dying of love!

She of the beautiful semblance
bade him shake the tambourine.
   Lovely, I'm dying of love!

Bade him strike the tambourine,
and they didn't allow him leisure.
   Lovely, I'm dying of love!

Bade him shake the tambourine,
and they didn't allow him to loiter.
   Lovely, I'm dying of love!

Meen Rodrigues Tenoiro

CV 318, CB 717, N 152

"My friend, because you tell me
that you're very much in love with me,
since now you go away from here,
tell me, what will you do?"
  "My lovely lady, I will tell you true:
  I shall soon return or I shall die."

"If our Lord will pardon you,
since you are grieving even here,
when you have gone far away, say,
by God, what will you do then?"
  "My lovely lady, I will tell you true:
  I shall soon return or I shall die."

Meendinho

CV 438, CB 852, N 252

I was at the chapel of Saint Simon,
and enormous waves surrounded me,
while awaiting my friend,
while awaiting my friend!

I was in the chapel, before the altar.
There surrounded me enormous waves of the sea,
while awaiting my friend,
while awaiting my friend!

And enormous waves surrounded me.
I have neither oarsman nor boatman,
while awaiting my friend,
while awaiting my friend!

There surrounded me enormous waves of the sea.
I have no oarsman, nor can I row,
while awaiting my friend,
while awaiting my friend!

I have neither oarsman nor boatman.
Lovely, I'll die in the depths of the sea,
while awaiting my friend,
while awaiting my friend!

I have no oarsman, nor can I row.
Lovely, I'll die in the grasp of the sea,
while awaiting my friend,
while awaiting my friend!

The birds, from Bartholomaeus Anglicus, *Boeck van den Proprieteyten der Dingen*, Haarlem, 1485.

Nuno Fernandez Torneol

cv 242, cb 641, n 75

Get up, my friend, who would sleep away the chilly dawns.
All the birds of the world were chattering of love.
Joyful am I.

Get up, my friend, who would sleep away the dawns so chill.
All the birds of the world were caroling of love.
Joyful am I.

All the birds of the world were chattering of love.
They were mindful in their songs of my love and yours.
Joyful am I.

All the birds of the world were caroling of love.
They remembered in their songs my love and yours.
Joyful am I.

They were mindful in their songs of my love and yours.
You took from them the branches on which they used to sit.
Joyful am I.

They were mindful in their songs of my love and yours.
You took from them the branches on which they used to perch.
Joyful am I.

You took from them the branches on which they used to sit.
You dried for them the fountains from which they used to drink.
Joyful am I.

You took from them the branches on which they used to perch.
You dried for them the fountains in which they used to bathe.
Joyful am I.

Nuno Fernandez Torneol

CV 245, CB 644, N 78

How very great my grief in suffering
for the love of a friend whom I do not see!
But I shall wait beneath the hazel tree!

How very great my grief in what I endure
for the love of a friend and not to speak with him!
But I shall wait beneath the hazel tree!

For love of a friend whom I do not see
and dare not speak to him my suffering!
But I shall wait beneath the hazel tree!

For the love of a friend and not to speak with him,
nor dare to reveal to him my suffering!
But I shall wait beneath the hazel tree!

And dare not to tell to him my suffering,
nor have I leisure because of my love for him.
But I shall wait beneath the hazel tree!

And dare not to show to him my suffering,
nor may I linger because of my love for him.
But I shall wait beneath the hazel tree!

Nuno Fernandez Torneol

CV 246, CB 645, N 79

I saw, my mother, the ships
afloat upon the sea,
and I am dying of love.

I went, my mother, to see
the ships upon the strand,
and I am dying of love.

The ships afloat in the sea
I went to await there,
and I am dying of love.

The ships upon the strand.
I went to wait for them,
and I am dying of love.

I went to await the ships
and could not find him there,
and I am dying of love.

I went to wait for the ships
and could not see him there,
and I am dying of love.

I did not find there him
whom I saw to my woe,
and I am dying of love.

I did not find him there,
the one I saw to my woe,
and I am dying of love.

Nuno Perez Sandeu

CV 384, CB 800, N 213

"Ah, daughter, he who loved you
swore to it the other day
but has not come to see you."
   "Ah, mother, he was afraid of you
      who treat me badly because of him."

"He who was pining for you
was certainly in the village here
but has not come to see you."
   "Ah, mother, he was frightened of you
      who treat me badly because of him."

"He who was pining for you
was proven a liar here today
and has not come to see you."
   "Ah, mother, he didn't dare because of you
      who treat me badly because of him."

Nuno Porco

CV 719, CB 1127, N 349

I shall go to the sea to see my friend.
I'll ask him if he wishes to live with me.
As his beloved I go.

I shall go to the sea to see my love.
I'll ask him if he will do just as I wish.
As his beloved I go.

I'll ask him why he doesn't live with me.
I'll tell him how I live and suffer for him.
As his beloved I go.

I'll ask him why he's displeased with me.
If he's angry with me, he wrongs me all in vain.
As his beloved I go.

Paio Calvo

CV 842, CB 1237, N 450

That liar of mine has gone
and sent no message to me.
    I'll long for him.

Ah, mother, he whom I loved
has gone on his way from here.
    I'll long for him.

And he's sent no message to me.
May God seek him for me!
    I'll long for him.

Since he's sent no message to me,
may Mary seek it from him!
    I'll long for him.

Paio de Cana

CV 522, CB 934, N 273

My friend, I knew that your lover
would not lie to you,
since he had sworn that he
would come, but I tell you
    that he is much afraid of you;
    that's why he has not sooner come.

And he asked that I see you
and bring a message to you,
that he was never false
and something else he said:
    that he is much afraid of you;
    that's why he has not sooner come.

And I wish for you, my friend,
that you have the best of luck,
and that you thank him much,
since he asked me to tell you
    that he is much afraid of you;
    that's why he has not sooner come.

Paio Gomez Charinho

cv 424, cb 838, n 221

They told me today, my friend, that
my lover's no longer an admiral of
the sea; now my heart can be
at peace; now it can sleep, and for this reason
    may God relieve of the pain that he suffers
    the one who removed my friend from the sea.

It's wonderful for me, because
I'll no longer sorrow to see the rise
of the wind, nor from storms lose
my sleep, but if it was the King himself—
    may God relieve of the pain that he suffers
    the one who removed my friend from the sea.

It's wonderful for me, because
each time a man arrives from the border,
I need not fear bad news, but since,
gratuitously, he benefited me,
    may God relieve of the pain that he suffers
    the one who removed my friend from the sea.

Printer's mark of Mathias Goes, Antwerp.

Paio Gomez Charinho

CV 401, CB 817, N 220

The flowers for my friend
go brilliantly on his ship,
and there sail the flowers
from here truly with my love.
Gone are the flowers
from here truly with my love.

The flowers for my lover
go brilliantly in his boat,
and there go the flowers
from here truly with my love.
Gone are the flowers
from here truly with my love.

Brilliant, they go on his ship
to arrive at the battleground,
and there go the flowers
from here truly with my love.
Gone are the flowers
from here truly with my love.

Brilliant, they go in his boat
to arrive at the soldiers' offensive,
and there go the flowers
from here truly with my love.
Gone are the flowers
from here truly with my love.

To arrive at the battleground
to serve me, my beautiful limbs,
and there go the flowers
from here truly with my love.

Gone are the flowers
from here truly with my love.

To arrive at the soldiers' offensive
to serve me, my lovely limbs,
and there go the flowers
from here truly with my love.
Gone are the flowers
from here truly with my love.

Paio Soarez de Taveiroos

CV 241, CB 640, N 74

When my friend went away,
he swore that he would come soon,
but he has not come to speak with me.
For that transgression, to Holy Mary
    never pray for him, my ladies,
    on my behalf, whatever you do!

When he went, he made
a promise to me to come very soon,
but he lied to me. A wrong was done,
and since he has no fear of me,
    never pray for him, my ladies,
    on my behalf, whatever you do!

O you who saw
that he said that he was in love, since
he did not come on the day that I
had sent for him to come to me,
    never pray for him, my ladies,
    on my behalf, whatever you do!

Paio Soarez de Taveiroos

cv 239, cb 638, n 72

My friend used to say to me
that never more would he live with me.
    By God, my ladies, here already he is!

After he had sworn to me
that he'd not see me more, by grace
    of God, my ladies, here already he is!

He who swore that he'd not see me,
but despite everything he said,
    by God, my ladies, here already he is!

Better was the deed than the threat that he'd made.
By God, my ladies, here already he is!

Pedro Eanes Solaz

CV 415, CB 829, N 236

I, the lovely one, didn't sleep,
    lelia doura,
but my friend was wont to come to me,
    e doi lelia doura.[3]

I didn't sleep and was always grieved,
    lelia doura,
but my friend was wont to arrive for me,
    e doi lelia doura.

My friend was wont to come to me,
    lelia doura,
and he'd speak so beautifully of love,
    e doi lelia doura.

And my friend was wont to arrive for me,
    lelia doura,
and he'd sing so beautifully of love,
    e doi lelia doura.

I ardently desired, my friend,
    lelia doura,
that you would be together with me,
    e doi lelia doura.

3. On this mysterious refrain see B. Dutton, "Lelia Doura, Edoy Lelia Doura: An Arabic Refrain in a Thirteenth-Century Galician Poem?," *Bulletin of Hispanic Studies* 41 (1964): 1–9. Dutton suggests as a possible translation, "The night [weighs] long [upon] me, / I languish, and the night [weighs] long [upon] me" or "My night drags on [wearisomely], / I languish and my night drags on [wearisomely]."

I ardently desired, my love,
    lelia doura,
that you would be close at my side,
    e doi lelia doura.

Leli, leli, by God, leli,
    lelia doura,
I know very well who doesn't say leli,
    e doi lelia doura.

I know very well who doesn't say leli,
    lelia doura.
A demon is he who doesn't say leli,
    e doi lelia doura.

Pero Garcia Burgalês

CV 251, CB 650, N 84

Do you not remember,
my friend, the wrong you did to me?
You proposed to speak with me.
I went, but you did not arrive:
    and you seek to speak with me?
    But I do not so seek, my friend.

You swore in every way that you
would come to me, willingly,
before the day was over and done.
You lied to me, you perjurer:
    and you seek to speak with me?
    But I do not so seek, my friend.

And yet you dare to ask me now
that I converse with you, my friend?
But, for what you did to me,
I declare I know you not:
    and you seek to speak with me?
    But I do not so seek, my friend.

Pero Garcia Burgalês

CV 250, CB 649, N 83

Ah, Mother, I tell you well,
my lover lied to me.
I am angry with him.

About what he'd sworn to me;
but since he willingly lied,
I am angry with him.

He didn't go where he should have gone,
but certainly from that day,
I am angry with him.

He is not parted from me,
but since he lied to me,
I am angry with him.

Pero Gonçalvez de Portocarreiro

cv 507, cb 920, n 262

My friend's ring
I lost beneath the verdant pine,
and I weep, pretty me.

My lover's ring
I lost beneath the verdant bough,
and I weep, pretty me.

I lost it beneath the verdant pine,
and I, the noble damsel, weep for it,
and I weep, pretty me.

I lost it beneath the verdant bough,
and I, the noble damsel, weep for it,
and I weep, pretty me.

Pero Gonçalvez de Portocarreiro

CV 505, CB 918, N 260

By God, I'm constantly grieved,
since my lover does not come.
Since he does not come, what shall I do?
   My locks, with silk
   I shall not bind you.

Since he does not come from Castile,
he's probably dead, ah wretched me,
or else the king detains him from me.
   My coifs from Estela,
   I shall not wear you.

Although I seem content,
I know no counsel to give myself.
My confidantes, what shall I do?
   In you, my mirror,
   I shall not look.

Those very pretty gifts
he gave to me, ah, my damsels,
I'll not deny the fact to you.
   My buckled belts,
   I shall not clasp you.

Pero Meogo

CV 797, CB 1192, N 419

"Tell me, my daughter, my pretty daughter,
  why you lingered at the chilly fountainhead?"
      I am in love.

"Tell me, daughter, my lovely daughter,
  why you lingered at the chilly fountainhead?"
      I am in love.

"I lingered, my mother, at the fountainhead chill.
  Deer from the mountain were troubling the water."
      I am in love.

"I lingered, my mother, at the chilly fountainhead.
  Deer from the mountain were muddying the water."
      I am in love.

"You lie, my laugher, because of your friend.
  I've never seen a deer trouble the brook."
      I am in love.

"You lie, my daughter, about your lover.
  I've never seen a deer muddy the stream."
      I am in love.

Pero Meogo

CV 796, CB 1191, N 418

Daughter, you went to the dance,
and there you tore your dress;
    since the stag comes there,
    approach the fountain with care,
    since the stag comes there.

Daughter, you went to the ball,
and there you tore your gown;
    since the stag comes there,
    approach the fountain with care,
    since the stag comes there.

And there you tore your dress,
which you made in my despite;
    since the stag comes there,
    approach the fountain with care,
    since the stag comes there.

And there you tore your gown,
which you made in my despite;
    since the stag comes there,
    approach the fountain with care,
    since the stag comes there.

Pero Meogo

CV 792, CB 1187, N 414

O stags of the hill, I've come to ask you,
my lover has gone and if he lingers there,
    what shall I do, my pretty ones?

O stags of the hill, I've come to tell you,
my friend has gone and now I'd like to know,
    what shall I do, my pretty ones?

Pero Meogo

CV 793, CB 1188, N 415

The lovely girl arose.
She goes to wash her hair
at the fountainhead's chill.
     So happily in love;
     in love so happily!

The lovely girl arose.
She goes to wash her hair
at the chilly fountainhead.
     So happily in love;
     in love so happily!

She goes to wash her hair
at the fountainhead's chill.
Her friend passed by
who loved her well.
     So happily in love;
     in love so happily!

She goes to wash her hair
at the chilly fountainhead.
Her friend passed by
who loved her much.
     So happily in love;
     in love so happily!

Her friend passed by
who loved her well.
The stag from the mountain
muddied the water.
     So happily in love;
     in love so happily!

Her friend passed by
who loved her much.
The stag from the mountain
troubled the water.
　　So happily in love;
　　in love so happily!

Pero Meogo

CV 794, CB 1189, N 416

In the green grasses
I saw the wandering does,
    my friend.

In the green meadows
I saw the stalwart stags,
    my friend.

Delighted with the does,
I washed my locks,
    my friend.

Delighted with the stags,
I washed my hair,
    my friend.

After I washed my locks,
I bound them with gold,
    my friend.

After I'd washed my hair,
I bound it with gold,
    my friend.

With gold I bound it
and waited for you,
    my friend,

With gold I'd bound them
and waited for you,
    my friend.

Pero Meogo

CV 791, CB 1186, N 413

So stricken is my friend
with the love I inspired in him,
he's like a stag wounded
by the huntsman of the king.

So stricken is my friend,
mother, with love of me,
he's like a stag wounded
by the huntsman of first degree.

If the stag is wounded,
it will go to die at the sea.
My friend will do the same
if I don't nurse his wound.

Take care, my daughter, for
I've seen such in my time,
who pretended to be grieved
that he might win my love.

Take care, my daughter, for
I've seen in my time such,
who pretended to be grieved
that my love he might win.

Pero da Ponte

CV 417, CB 831, N 238

Did you see, mother, the squire
who is to take me off with him?
I lied to him, he's angry with me,
my mother, I tell you truly so.
    Mother, he left me in love with him.
    Mother, he's left me in love with him.
    Mother, he left me in love with him.

Mother, you who commanded me
to lie to my beloved friend,
what counsel do you give me now
that I'm no longer together with him?
    Mother, he left me in love with him.
    Mother, he's left me in love with him.
    Mother, he left me in love with him.

Daughter, I counsel you now that
the moment that he sees you,
you do everything for him
that he be satisfied with you.
    Mother, he left me in love with him.
    Mother, he's left me in love with him.
    Mother, he left me in love with him.

Since you are not able to live without,
my daughter, his consoling presence,
from this day forth I advise you
that you do for him what he commands.
    Mother, he left me in love with him.
    Mother, he's left me in love with him.
    Mother, he left me in love with him.

Pero da Ponte

CV 420, CB 834, N 241

My friend has gone away from here
to join the army to serve the king,
and never since have I been able
to sleep, but I'm happy enough that
    since he keeps me waiting, and does not come,
    it is the king who keeps him from me.

But I shall not be relieved of my great grief
in the least unless I see him, for
my heart is not tranquil enough for that,
although this much comfort I have:
    since he keeps me waiting, and does not come,
    it is the king who keeps him from me.

But he ought to remind himself of the vows
that he swore to me then and there where he
abandoned me, his pretty girl,
but, my damsels, you can swear:
    since he keeps me waiting, and does not come,
    it is the king who keeps him from me.

Pero Viviaez

CV 336, CB 735, N 169

Since our mothers go to San Simon
of Val de Prados to burn candles,
let us, the daughters try to go
with our mothers there, and let them
burn candles for us and for themselves,
and we, the daughters, will dance there.

All our friends will go there
to see us, and we shall dance before
them, beautiful, without a cloak,
and let our mothers, since they go there,
burn candles for us and for themselves,
and we, the daughters, will dance there.

Our friends will go to admire there
how we dance and be able to see
pretty young girls dancing there,
and let our mothers, since they wish to go,
burn candles for us and for themselves,
and we, the daughters, will dance there.

Sancho Sanchez

CV 525, CB 937, N 275

My dear, I've had a message
from my friend and tell you truly
that he lives and loves another,
    but I swear to God I'd rather
    have heard that he had died.

I was surprised that he
had tarried so long because
I've always supposed that I'd
have my vengeance of him,
    but I swear to God I'd rather
    have heard that he had died.

Though I lived in pain, now
I know not what I'll do,
since he desires another
and abandons me whom he served,
    but I swear to God I'd rather
    have heard that he had died.

And it would be much better for him
and give me greater pleasure by far.

Sancho Sanchez

CV 524, CB 936, N 274

My friend, well do I know that my beloved
is either dead or loves another lady,
for he's sent no message to me, nor does he come,
but when he left, he made a promise to me
    that he would come soon and of good will
    or else send a message to me.

It grieved me very much when he went away,
and I began at that time to question him:
do you intend, my love, to linger there long?
He swore to me by Holy Mary then
    that he would come soon and of good will
    or else send a message to me.

And then while he was speaking with me, I said
to him: what will I do if you do not come
or if I do not receive a message soon
from you? And then he wept and swore to me
    that he would come soon and of good will
    or else send a message to me.

Vaasco Gil

CV 266, CB 664, N 98

Sister, my friend,
he who loves me very much
and who is passionate for me,
if our Lord will forgive you,
    arrange, my sister, for my friend
    to come together with me.

Sister, my friend
who, I know, desires me more
than himself or his own heart—
do this one thing for me:
    arrange, my sister, for my friend
    to come together with me.

Sister, my friend
who, I know, desires me more
than his own eyes and dies for me—
may God lead your lover to you—
    arrange my sister, for my friend
    to come together with me.

Vaasco Praga de Sandim

CV 236, CB 634, N 69

You may suppose, my friend,
that I don't love you very much,
but never may I fare well
if I see a thing in the world
    that takes from me desire for you
    when you are out of view.

Although you so suppose,
I have such enormous love
in my heart for you, my friend,
that I know no thing in the world
    that takes from me desire for you
    when you are out of view.

And may you never love
me well, for it would be death,
if you knew, my friend, that I
had found a thing in the world
    that takes from me desire for you
    when you are out of view.

Afonso Eanes do Coton. *Segrel* of the latter half of the thirteenth century. He has been described as a womanizer, gambler, and heavy drinker. He is said to have been killed by his drinking companion, Pero da Ponte, who stole his poems, but this probably is not true.

Afonso Lopes de Baiam. *Trovador*. A nobleman who held positions as governor in the latter half of the thirteenth century, he wrote poems of all three types that have come down to us from medieval Portugal.

Afonso Sanches (1289–1329). The illegitimate and favorite son of King Dinis, he wrote *cantigas de amor* and *cantigas de amigo*.

Airas Corpancho. Probably a Galician *jogral* before the time of Afonso III (1248–79), he wrote *cantigas de amor* and *cantigas de amigo*. "Corpancho," which means "broad body," is undoubtedly a satirical nickname of the sort often given to *jograls*.

Airas Nunes de Santiago. Thought to be Galician, he was called *clerigo*, probably because of his learning, not because he actually held an ecclesiastical position. He may have been educated, at least in part, in France, and he served at the Castilian court of Sancho IV (1258–95). Poetically active between 1280 and 1290, he wrote poems of all three types.

Bernal de Bonaval. Galician *Segrel*. Active in the courts of Fernando III (1217–52) and Alfonso X (1252–84), he wrote *cantigas de amor* and *cantigas de amigo*.

Dom Dinis. King of Portugal (1279–1325). He founded the first Portuguese university, developed agriculture and forestry, increased the size of the navy, and fortified towns. One of the best of the medieval poets, he composed poems of all three types.

Estevam Coelho. One of the last poets of King Dinis's reign. Two of his *cantigas* have survived. Thought to be the grandson of the *trovador* Joam Soarez Coelho, he may also have been the brother of Pero Coelho, one of the murderers of Dom Pedro's mistress, Inés de Castro.

Fernan Frojaz. Active in the latter half of the thirteenth century, he wrote *cantigas de amigo*.

Fernan Gonçalvez de Seabra. *Trovador* of the reign of Afonso III. He wrote *cantigas de amor* and *cantigas de amigo*.

Fernan Rodriguez de Calheiros. Probably flourished in the latter half of the thirteenth century. He wrote poems of all three types, but his *cantigas de amigo* are his best.

Fernando Esquio (i.e., "lank"). May have been one of the last of the *trovadores* and a member of the lower ranks of the Galician nobility or an obscure *jogral* during the reign of King Dinis. He wrote poems of all three types.

Joam Airas de Santiago. *Trovador*. He frequented the court of Afonso III or Dinis and wrote poems of all three types.

Joam d'Avoin. A nobleman who held offices at court, he died at the end of the thirteenth century. He wrote poems of all three types.

Joam Baveca. Galician *jogral* or *segrel* at the court of Alfonso X. He wrote poems of all three types.

Joam de Cangas. *Jogral*. He wrote *cantigas de amigo*.

Joam Garcia Guilhade. *Trovador*. He served at the court of Alfonso X and wrote poems of all three types.

Joam Lopez d'Ulhoa. A nobleman, perhaps a contemporary of Afonso III. He wrote *cantigas de amor* and *cantigas de amigo*.

Joam Nunes Camanez. Wrote *cantigas de amor* and *cantigas de amigo*.

Joam Servando. *Jogral*. He wrote all three types of poetry.

Joam Soarez Coelho. Portuguese nobleman. Active between 1250 and 1279, he fought under Afonso III. He wrote poems of all three types.

Joam Zorro (i.e., "sly"). *Jogral*, probably of Portuguese extraction. Active in the late thirteenth century, perhaps at the court of Dinis, he wrote one *cantiga de amor* and ten *cantigas de amigo*, especially *barcarolas*.

Juliâo Bolseiro. *Jogral* from Galicia or Portugal. He was active at the courts of Alfonso X and Afonso III. Although he is known chiefly for his *cantigas de amigo*, two of his *cantigas de amor* and two of his *cantigas de escarnho e de mal dizer* survive.

Lopo. *Jogral.* Working in the period before 1250, he wrote *cantigas de amor* and *cantigas de amigo*.

Lourenço. Portuguese *jogral.* He wrote poems of all three types in the latter half of the thirteenth century. His pretensions to the title of *trovador* earned him ridicule in *cantigas de escarnho e de mal dizer* of the period.

Martin Codax. Galician *jogral.* Active in the middle of the thirteenth century, he was the author of seven lovely *cantigas de amigo* that refer to the sea.

Martin de Ginzo. *Jogral.* As far as is known, he wrote only *cantigas de amigo*.

Meen Rodrigues Tenoiro. He was perhaps a nobleman who died in 1360 or an earlier member of the same family who flourished in the mid-thirteenth century.

Meendinho. *Jogral.* Only one *cantiga de amigo* that he wrote has survived.

Nuno Fernandez Torneol. Perhaps a *segrel.* Probably a knight, he was a contemporary of Afonso III. He wrote poems of all three types.

Nuno Perez Sandeu. Nothing is known of him beyond the fact that he was the author of several *cantigas de amigo*.

Nuno Porco (i.e., "pig"). *Jogral*, perhaps of the late twelfth century. He wrote *cantigas de amor* and *cantigas de amigo*.

Paio Calvo. Probably a *jogral.* Two of his *cantigas de amigo* survive.

Paio de Cana. Probably a priest who worked in the middle of the thirteenth century. He wrote *cantigas de amigo*.

Paio Gomez Charinho. A nobleman, Admiral of Castile under Alfonso X and his son. He wrote poems of all three types.

Paio Soarez de Taveiroos. Nobleman. Active in the early thirteenth century and perhaps also at the end of the twelfth, he wrote *cantigas de amor* and *cantigas de amigo*.

Pedro Eanes Solaz. *Jogral.* Wrote *cantigas de amor* and *cantigas de amigo*. He was perhaps a contemporary of Afonso III.

Pero Garcia Burgalês. Wrote poems of all three types. He is known to have visited the court of Afonso III.

Pero Gonçalvez de Portocarreiro. Perhaps a nobleman. He wrote *cantigas de amigo*.

Pero Meogo. *Jogral*. Perhaps a monk or former monk, he wrote nine *cantigas de amigo*, seven of which use the motif of the deer at the fountain.

Pero da Ponte. *Segrel* at the court of Alfonso X. He wrote poems of all three types.

Pero Viviaez. *Jogral*. He wrote poems of all three types.

Sancho Sanchez. *Trovador*. He was a member of the clergy.

Vaasco Gil. Nobleman. Active in the latter half of the thirteenth century, he wrote poems of all three types.

Vaasco Praga de Sandim. Probably flourished in the early thirteenth century. He wrote *cantigas de amor* and *cantigas de amigo*.